T0096898

RUM
cocktails

STUART WALTON

LORENZ BOOKS

Contents

Introduction

Of all the basic spirits, rum is probably still the least appreciated. Distilled from sugarcane throughout the Caribbean and Latin America, its story is inextricably bound up with maritime trade and a life on the ocean wave. Notoriously, it was one of the currencies that sustained the transportation of slaves from western Africa to the Americas, and it was, until 1970 at least, issued as a daily ration to British sailors serving in the Royal Navy. In the modern era, its popularity was boosted with the advent of package tours to the sun-soaked Caribbean islands, where a proliferating repertoire of tropical cocktails awaited the intrepid vacationer.

The Daiquiri, originally a simple white rum sour and as emblematic in cocktail history as the gin Martini, has been the inspiration for a whole generation of variations incorporating fruit liqueurs and matching fresh fruit purées. Blended with heaps of smashed ice, the drink became a frozen daiquiri, generally a sweeter and gentler proposition than the original.

There are three essential styles of rum, delineated according to their colours, which are determined by the length of time (if any) the rum has spent ageing in casks: white (of which the pre-eminent international brand is Bacardi); light or golden, a versatile halfway-house style; and dark or black, the woody, often treacly-tasting rums that are subjected to long barrel maturation. The top-strength naval rums known as 'overproof' are speciality products, good for adding in droplets to a cocktail mixture to concentrate its flavour.

Dedicated rum bars have sprung up in cities outside the drink's region of origin, but they are still very much a niche market compared to those for gin and vodka. A speciality style that is much enjoyed these days, and makes an excellent cocktail ingredient, is spiced rum, usually a golden style that contains infusions of anything from ginger, vanilla, nutmeg, cinnamon, cloves or allspice to bracing citrus notes from orange or lime.

Right: White rum with plenty of ice, mint and lime make the perfect Mojito; an essential drink at a barbecue.

What is rum?

Probably the least understood of the five main spirits, rum is actually, in its white version, one of the biggest-selling of them all. Indeed, it is debatable whether many of those knocking back Bacardi-and-Cokes realize they are drinking some form of rum at all. To many, rum is inextricably associated with a rather antiquated pantomime idea of "Jolly Jack Tars" and a life on the ocean wave.

There is some uncertainty over the origin of the spirit's name, but the favourite theory is that it is a shortening of an old West Country English word "rumbullion", itself of unknown origin, but generally denoting any hard liquor.

The invention of rum dates from not long after the foundation of the sugar plantations in the West Indies, in the early 16th century. Until the voyages of Christopher Columbus, sugar was a luxury product, and much sought after in southern Europe, having originally been brought into Venice from India. When the Spanish explorers landed in Hispaniola and the neighbouring Caribbean islands, they saw promising environments for cultivating sugar cane for themselves.

If yeasts need to feed on sugar in order to produce alcohol, then the sugar plant was always going to be an obvious candidate for distillation. When first pressed, cane juice is a murky, greenish colour and full of impurities. Boiled down, it crystallizes into sucrose and a sticky brown by-product, molasses, that would have fermented readily in tropical conditions. Rum is the result of distilling the fermented molasses.

Sugar soon became a widespread everyday product in Europe. The astronomical demand for it was serviced by the most notorious episode in European colonial history – the slave trade – in which rum played a crucial role. Settlers in New England financed their trips to West Africa by selling rum. A consignment of African slaves would be delivered to the

Above left: Wood's 100 is a rich naval strength dark rum.
Above right: Captain Morgan is one of the leading brands of dark rum.

West Indies and sold for molasses, which would then be shipped back to New England to be turned into more rum.

The association of rum with the British Navy arises from the fact that rum was provided to ordinary sailors – as a daily ration from the

18th century. That tradition endured, basically because rum could withstand hot weather more sturdily than beer could. The initial allowance was a fairly rollicking half-pint a day, watered down eventually into the despised "grog", and then mixed with lemon juice to prevent scurvy. It was only in 1970 that the rum ration was abolished.

Below left: Bacardi is the world's favourite white rum.
Below right: Mount Gay Barbados is a major brand of Caribbean golden rum.

Today, rum is produced all over the West Indies and eastern South America, to a lesser extent in the Indian Ocean area – the Philippines and Mauritius – and in smaller quantities still in the USA and Australia. Inevitably, much of it is a by-product of the sugar-refining industry, but the best grades are made by smaller, independent companies growing sugar cane specifically for distillation.

Some rum is made from the pressed cane juice itself, but most is made from fermented molasses. In the former French colonies in particular, there is a distinguished tradition of *rhum agricole*, speciality

Above: Cuba Libre is a classic cocktail that has Bacardi as its rum of choice.

products made on small sugar farms, produced with different strains of yeast.

Both methods of distillation are practised in the making of rum: the premium versions are double-distilled in a copper pot still, whereas continuous distillation and thorough rectification are used mainly by the bulk producers, particularly for the neutral-tasting white rums. Freshly distilled spirit from the pot still method is very high in impurities and needs to

Above: Kraken Rum, which was introduced in 2010, is just one of many brands to take advantage of the surge in popularity of golden spiced rum.

mellow through a period of cask-ageing, which gives colour to the darker rums.

After white rum, dark rum is the next most important category commercially, and is certainly where the superior products are found. Leading brands are Captain Morgan and Lamb's. Some high-quality dark rums are bottled at the original naval strength of more than 50% ABV (Wood's Navy Rum, for example, is 57%); the traditional name for such strengths was "overproof". The everyday dark rums are a more standard 40%, while Bacardi is adjusted down to 37.5%, equivalent to the other white spirits.

Between the two styles is the increasingly popular golden or light rum, which is a particular speciality of Cuba and Puerto Rico, aged for less time in the barrel. The darkest and heaviest rums, some not far from the colour of black treacle, traditionally come from Jamaica. Good white rum, such as the white Rhum St James of Martinique, is full of burnt-sugar richness. Some exporters make a virtue of selling rums with 30 or 40 years of cask age, and there is even a tiny production of vintage-dated rum for the true connoisseur.

How rum is made

Juice from the sugar cane is pressed and either fermented straight or boiled down to extract the molasses, which itself forms the basis of the ferment. It is either continuously distilled or, for speciality products, double-distilled in a pot still. For a headier product, some of the residue of the first distillation – known as "dunder" – may be added to the molasses during fermentation. Commercial white rums are rectified and bottled immediately. Coloured rums are cask-aged, sometimes for decades, before they are bottled. The longer they are aged in the cask, the deeper the colour.

How to serve

The best dark rums, and aged rums in particular, should be served straight, unchilled, as digestifs. They make stimulating alternatives to malt whisky or cognac. Premium white rums from the independent producers are also best enjoyed neat, but they should be served cold, with a twist of lime.

Of the commercial products, white rum mixes famously well with cola, but also with orange juice or more tropical flavours such as pineapple or mango. Dark rum has traditionally been seen as compatible with blackcurrant or peppermint cordials, as well as the ubiquitous cola.

However you prefer your rum remember to treat it with respect and always drink responsibly.

Right: A refreshing Mai Tai is the perfect long drink to enjoy on a hot summer's day.

Cocktail equipment

To be a successful bartender, you will need a few essential pieces of equipment. The most vital and flamboyant is the cocktail shaker.

Cocktail shaker: The shaker is used for drinks that need good mixing but don't have to be crystal-clear. The Boston shaker is made of two cup-type containers that fit over each other, one normally made of glass, the other of metal. This type is often preferred by professional bartenders. For beginners, the classic three-piece shaker is easier to handle, with its base to hold the ice and liquids, a top fitted with a built-in strainer, and a tight-fitting cap. Make sure you hold on to that cap while you are shaking. As a rough rule, the drink is ready when the shaker has become almost too painfully cold to hold, which is generally not more than around 15–20 seconds.

Measure or "jigger": Cocktail shakers usually come with a standard measure – known in American parlance as a "jigger" – for apportioning out the ingredients. This is usually a single-piece double cup, with one side a whole measure and the other a half.

Measuring jug and spoons: If you don't have a jigger, you can use a jug and/or a set of spoons. The measurements can be in single (25ml/1fl oz) or double (50ml/2fl oz) bar measures.

Blender or liquidizer: Goblet blenders are the best shape for mixing cocktails that need to be aerated, as well as for creating frothy cocktails or ones made with finely crushed ice. Attempting to break up whole ice cubes in the blender may very well blunt the blades. Opt for an ice bag or dish towel, a rolling pin and plenty of brute force, or better still, use an ice crusher.

Ice crusher: This comes in two parts. You fill the top with whole ice cubes, put the lid on and, while pressing down on the top, turn the gramophone-type handle on the side. Take the top half off to retrieve the crystals of ice "snow" from the lower part. Crushed ice is used to fill the glasses for drinks that are to be served frappé. It naturally melts very quickly, though, compared to cubes.

Wooden hammer: Use a wooden hammer or wooden rolling pin for crushing ice.

Towel or ice bag A clean towel or bag is essential for holding ice cubes when crushing.

Ice bucket: An ice bucket is useful if you are going to be making several cocktails in succession. They are not completely hermetic though, and ice will eventually melt in them, albeit a little more slowly than if left at room temperature.

Mixing pitcher or bar glass: It is useful to have a container in which to mix and stir drinks that are not shaken. The pitcher or bar glass should be large enough to hold two or three drinks. This vessel is intended for drinks that are meant to be clear, not cloudy.

Bar spoon: These long-handled spoons can reach to the bottom of the tallest tumblers and are used in jugs, or for mixing the drink directly in the glass. Some varieties of bar spoon look like a large swizzle-stick, with a long spiral-shaped handle and a disc at one end.

Muddler: A long stick with a bulbous end, the muddler is used for crushing sugar or mint leaves, and so is particularly useful when creating juleps or smashes. A variety of sizes is available.

Strainer: Used for pouring drinks from a shaker or mixing jug into a cocktail glass, the strainer's function is to remove the ice with which the drink has been prepared. The best-known is called a Hawthorn strainer. It is made from stainless steel and looks like a flat spoon with holes and a curl of wire on the underside. It is held over the top of the glass to keep the ice and any other solid ingredients back.

Corkscrew: The fold-up type of corkscrew is known as the Waiter's Friend, and incorporates a can opener and bottle-top flipper as well as the screw itself. It is the most useful version to have to hand.

Sharp knife and squeezer: Citrus fruit is essential in countless cocktails. A good quality, sharp knife is required for halving the fruit, and the squeezer for extracting its juice.

Nutmeg grater: A tiny grater with small holes, for grating nutmeg over frothy and creamy drinks.

Zester and canelle knife: These are used for presenting fruit attractively to garnish glasses. The zester has a row of tiny holes that remove the top layer of skin off a citrus fruit when dragged across it (although the finest gauge on your multi-purpose grater was also designed for just this job).

A canelle knife is for making decorative stripes in the skins of a whole fruit. When sliced, they then have an attractive serrated edge.

Egg whisk: Use a whisk to beat a little frothy texture into egg white

Above: You can amass cocktail equipment over time.

before you add it to the shaker. It helps the texture of the drink.

Cocktail and swizzle-sticks: Cocktail sticks are mainly decorative, used for holding ingredients such as olives that would otherwise sink to the bottom of the glass. And if you intend to eat the olive, it's handier if it's already speared, so that you don't have to commit the appalling faux pas of dipping a finger into the drink to catch it. A swizzle-stick is useful for stirring a drink, and may be substituted by a stick of celery or cucumber.

Glasses

To ensure that glasses are sparkling clean, they should always be washed and dried with a glass cloth. Although some recipes suggest chilled glasses, don't put best crystal in the freezer; leave it at the back of the refrigerator instead. An hour should be enough.

Collins glass

The tallest of the tumblers, narrow with perfectly straight sides, a Collins glass holds about 350ml/

Left: Collins glass

12fl oz, and is usually used for serving long drinks made with fresh juices or finished with a sparkling mixer such as soda. This glass can also stand in as the highball glass, which is traditionally slightly less tall. Uses: Mai Tai, Escape Route, Sun City, and all drinks that are to be "topped up" with anything.

Cocktail glass or Martini glass

This elegant glass is a wide conical bowl on a tall stem: a design that keeps cocktails cool by keeping warm hands away from the drink. It is by far the most widely used glass, so a set is essential. The design belies the fact that the capacity of this glass is relatively small (about three standard measures). Uses: The classic Daiquiri and its variations, and almost any short, sharp, strong cocktail, including creamy ones.

Left: Cocktail glass or Martini glass

Above: Tumbler or rocks glass and liqueur glass

Tumbler or rocks glass

Classic, short whisky tumblers are used for shorter drinks, served on the rocks, and generally for drinks that are stirred rather than shaken. They should hold about 250ml/8fl oz. Uses: Presidente, Passion Punch, Beach Peach and Jamaica Sunday.

Liqueur glass

Tiny liqueur glasses were traditionally used to serve small measures of unmixed drinks, and hold no more than 80ml/3fl oz. Uses: Straight fine rum, dark or golden, served ice cold.

Above: Large cocktail goblet and champagne saucer.

Large cocktail goblet
Available in various sizes and shapes, large cocktail goblets are good for serving larger frothy drinks, or drinks containing puréed fruit or coconut cream. The wider rim of this type of glass leaves plenty of room for flamboyant and colourful decorations. Uses: Chop Nut, Havana Bandana and Hustler.

Champagne saucer
The old-fashioned saucer glass may be frowned on now for champagne, but it is an attractive and elegant design and can be used for a number of cocktails, particularly

those that have cracked ice floating in them. Because of the wider surface are, there is plenty of scope for fruity garnishes too. Uses: Between the Sheets, Waikiki Beach and Angel's Treat.

Shot glass
A tiny glass with a capacity of no more than 50ml/2fl oz, the shot glass is used for those very short, lethally strong cocktails known as shooters. If you're going to make a shooter, this is absolutely the only glass to use. No substitute will be accepted. The glass itself is usually extremely thick, as these drinks are intended to be thrown back in one, and then the glass slammed down fairly peremptorily on the bar counter. Uses: Straight rum – whatever the colour – go for it!

Right: Shot glass

Tricks of the trade

It is worth mastering the techniques for the preparation of good-looking drinks. The following pages give you precise directions for some of the essential procedures, such as crushing ice and shaking cocktails.

Crushing ice

It isn't a good idea to break ice up in a blender or food processor as you may find it damages the blades. Instead do the following:

1 Lay out a clean glass cloth or dish towel, on a work surface, and cover half of it with ice cubes. (If you wish, you can also use a cloth ice bag.)

2 Fold the cloth over and, using a rolling pin or mallet, smash down on the ice firmly several times, until you achieve the required fineness.

3 Spoon the ice into glasses or a pitcher. Fine ice snow must be used immediately because it melts, but cracked or roughly crushed ice can be stored in the freezer in plastic bags.

Shaking cocktails

Cocktails that contain sugar syrups or creams require more than just a stir; they are combined and chilled with a brief shake. Remember that it is possible to shake only one or two servings at any one time, so you may have to work quickly in batches. It is important to always use fresh ice each time.

1 Add four or five ice cubes to the shaker and pour in all the ingredients.

2 Put the lid on the shaker. Hold the shaker firmly in one hand, keeping the lid in place with the other hand.

3 Shake vigorously for about 15 seconds to blend simple concoctions, and for 20–30 seconds for drinks with sugar syrups or cream. The shaker should feel extremely cold.

4 Remove the small cap and pour into the prepared glass, using a strainer if the shaker is not already fitted with one.

Frosting glasses

The appearance and taste of a cocktail are enhanced if the rim of your glass is frosted. After frosting, place the glass in the refrigerator to chill until needed.

1 Hold the glass upside down, so the juice does not run down the glass. Rub the rim with the cut surface of a lemon, lime, orange or even a slice of fresh pineapple.

2 Keeping the glass upside down, dip the rim into a shallow layer of sugar, coconut or salt. Redip the glass, if necessary, and turn it so that the rim is well-coated.

3 Stand the glass upright and let it sit until the sugar, coconut or salt has dried on the rim, then chill.

Making twists

As an alternative to slices of the fruit, drinks can be garnished with a twist of orange, lemon or lime rind. Twists should be made before the drink itself is prepared, so that you don't keep a cold cocktail waiting. Here's how:

1 Choose a citrus fruit with an unblemished skin and a regular shape.

2 Using a canelle knife or potato peeler, start at the tip of the fruit and start peeling round, as though you were peeling an apple.

3 Work slowly and carefully down the fruit, being sure to keep the pared-away rind in one continuous strip.

4 Trim it, if necessary, to a length that suits the glass.

5 A long twist in a cocktail glass makes the drink look sophisticated and elegant, and can be enhanced by the addition of a slice of the same fruit on the rim of the glass.

the cocktails

Tom and Jerry

A cold weather drink invented in the 1850s by the legendary Jerry Thomas of St Louis, Missouri, Tom and Jerry is one of the oldest cocktails in this book. It is said that Mr Thomas would traditionally serve these warming drinks at the first snows of winter. This recipe serves four to six people.

For the batter:

3 eggs
45ml/3 tbsp caster (superfine) sugar
pinch bicarbonate of soda (baking soda)
1 measure/1½ tbsp dark rum
1.5ml/¼ tsp ground cinnamon
pinch ground cloves
pinch allspice

Separate the eggs and beat the whites into stiff peaks, adding 15ml/1 tbsp of the sugar with the bicarbonate. Mix the yolks separately with the rum, the rest of the sugar and the spices. Then fold in the whites with a metal spoon.

For each drink:

1 measure/1½ tbsp dark rum
1 measure/1½ tbsp brandy
4 measures/6 tbsp boiling milk

Using heatproof glasses, put in 15ml/1 tbsp of the batter and 1 measure/1½ tbsp each of rum and brandy, then top up with boiled milk. Dust with nutmeg.

Bacardi Cocktail

In the original recipe, this must (legally, in the USA) be made with the world's biggest-selling white rum brand. It's short and sour and altogether perfect.

1½ measures/2 tbsp Bacardi white rum
juice of half a lime
¼ measure/1 tsp grenadine

Shake all the ingredients well with ice, and strain into a cocktail glass. Add a slice of lime. (Add a measure of gin to turn it into a Bacardi Special, a variation created back in the 1920s.)

Daiquiri

The Daiquiri is one of the most adapted and abused cocktails in the repertoire. Created in the 1890s, it is named after a town in Cuba and was originally nothing more than a white rum sour. Despite its extreme simplicity, this really is one of the all-time perfect cocktail recipes, standing proud above the more fashionable fruit versions.

2 measures/3 tbsp white rum
juice of half a lime or a quarter of a
*   lemon*
5ml/1 tsp caster (superfine) sugar

Shake all the ingredients well with ice to dissolve the sugar, and strain into a well-chilled cocktail glass. Serve ungarnished.

Strega Daiquiri

This is more or less a standard Daiquiri, in which the liqueur forms an additional element, rather than replacing the rum.

1 measure/1½ tbsp Strega
1 measure/1½ tbsp white rum
½ measure/2 tsp lemon juice
½ measure/2 tsp orange juice
2.5ml/½ tsp sugar syrup

Shake all the ingredients well with ice, and strain into a chilled cocktail glass. Garnish with a maraschino cherry.

Bartending know-how

To make home-made sugar syrup, gently heat 350g/12oz sugar and 600ml/1 pint water in a pan, stirring until the sugar has dissolved. Wipe the sides of the pan to remove any sugar crystals that might cause the syrup to crystallize. Bring to the boil for 3–5 minutes. Skim any scum away and when no more appears, remove the pan from the heat. Cool and pour into clean, dry, airtight bottles.

Cuba Libre

This is a brand-specific cocktail if ever there was one. Created in Cuba – where Bacardi was then produced – in the late 19th century, the novelty value of Cuba Libre lay in its use of Coca-Cola, a newfangled tonic beverage, then less than ten years on the market.

juice and rind of half a lime
2 measures/3 tbsp Bacardi white rum
5 measures/120ml/4 fl oz Coca-Cola

Squeeze the juice directly into a highball glass half-filled with cracked ice, and then put the empty rind in too. Add the rum, stir, and finally top up with ice-cold Coca-Cola. Garnish with a lime slice.

Caribbean Breeze

This bang-up-to-date mixture of exotic fruit flavours will have party guests coming back for more.

1½ measures/2 tbsp dark rum
½ measure/2 tsp crème de banane
3 measures/4½ tbsp pineapple
* juice*
2 measures/3 tbsp cranberry juice
¼ measure/1 tsp lime cordial

Shake all the ingredients well with ice, and strain into a large wine goblet, generously filled with crushed ice. Garnish with a slice of pineapple and a wedge of lime.

Planter's Punch

This long, refreshing, old colonial drink originates from the original sugar plantations that are dotted throughout the West Indian islands.

1 measure/1½ tbsp fresh lime juice
1 measure/1½ tbsp orange juice
2 measures/3 tbsp dark rum
½ measure/2 tsp grenadine
dash Angostura bitters
soda water or lemonade, chilled

Squeeze the lime and orange juices and add them to a pitcher of ice. Add the dark rum and the grenadine, and mix them together well for about 20 seconds. Add a dash of Angostura bitters to the bottom of a wide tumbler filled with cracked ice cubes. Strain the rum and grenadine mixture into the chilled tumbler. Finish with plenty of chilled soda water or lemonade, according to taste.

Garnish with two skewered peach slices and a physalis, complete with its leaves attached.

Mai Tai

This is a very refreshing, long but strong party drink that slides down easily – just before you do!

1 measure/1½ tbsp light rum
1 measure/1½ tbsp dark rum
1 measure/1½ tbsp apricot brandy
3 measures/4½ tbsp orange juice
3 measures/4½ tbsp pineapple juice
1 measure/1½ tbsp grenadine

Shake the first five ingredients well with ice, and strain into a highball glass half-filled with cracked ice. Slowly pour the grenadine into the glass, letting it sink to the bottom of the drink to make a glowing red layer. The cocktail could be lavishly garnished with tropical fruits.

Mary Pickford

A 1920s recipe in tribute to one of the greats among the first generation of silent movie stars.

1½ measures/2 tbsp white rum
1½ measures/2 tbsp pineapple juice
¼ measure/1 tsp grenadine
dash maraschino

Shake all the ingredients well with ice, and strain into a cocktail glass filled with crushed ice. Garnish with a maraschino cherry.

Bartending know-how
A recipe that calls for crushed ice sounds like hard work. If you are serving cocktails to a moderate-sized social gathering, you may have to stay up all night with a sledgehammer. Alternatively, just buy an ice crusher to do the work for you.

Columbus

A simple and appealing mixture of sweet and sour, Columbus must absolutely be made with light rum, but if that's the only colour you haven't got, use a half-and-half mixture of dark and white.

1½ measures/2 tbsp light rum
¾ measure/1 tbsp apricot brandy
1 measure/1½ tbsp lime juice

Shake all the ingredients well with ice, and strain into a cocktail glass. Garnish with slices of lime.

Presidente

Another 1920s Cuban recipe, this is named in honour of one of the island's old military rulers.

2 measures/3 tbsp white rum
1 measure/1½ tbsp orange curaçao
½ measure/2 tsp dry vermouth
¼ measure/1 tsp grenadine

Stir the ingredients with ice in a pitcher to chill them well, and then strain into a frozen rocks glass. Add a slice of lemon, decorated around the edges.

Waikiki Beach

This creamy, nutty, exotic cocktail has the power to call up memories of Caribbean beach holidays gone by.

1½ measures/2 tbsp white rum
½ measure/2 tsp amaretto
½ measure/2 tsp canned coconut
　cream
2 measures/3 tbsp pineapple juice
1 measure/1½ tbsp passion fruit
　juice
1 measure/1½ tbsp double (heavy)
　cream

Shake all the ingredients well with ice, and strain into a bowl-shaped cocktail glass half-filled with cracked ice. Garnish with a cube of pineapple and a maraschino cherry.

Bartending know-how
Cream cocktails should always be made with double (heavy) cream as the single (light) version tends to be too runny.

Saoco

I have drunk this cocktail on Barbados served in half a hollowed-out coconut shell, but it does nearly as well served in a plain glass tumbler. Coconut milk is the watery liquid that is released from the centre of a coconut when the end is pierced, and not to be confused with canned coconut cream.

2 measures/3 tbsp white rum
4 measures/6 tbsp coconut milk

Shake both the ingredients well with ice, and then strain into a rocks glass that has been half-filled with finely crushed ice. Drink through two short straws.

Bartending know-how
If serving in hollowed-out coconut shells, make sure they are thoroughly clean.

Blue Hawaiian

This drink can be decorated as flamboyantly as Carmen Miranda's headdress with a mixture of fruits and leaves. It is an eye-catching, colourful cocktail that you'll find very drinkable.

1 measure/1½ tbsp blue curaçao
1 measure/1½ tbsp coconut cream
2 measures/3 tbsp light rum
2 measures/3 tbsp pineapple juice
leaves and wedge of pineapple,
    slice of prickly pear or orange, a
    wedge of lime and a maraschino
    cherry, to garnish

Put the curaçao, coconut cream and light rum in a blender with a few cubes of ice. Process very briefly until the colour is even. Add the pineapple juice to the blender and process the mixture once more until frothy. Spoon crushed ice into a large cocktail glass or goblet until three-quarters full. Strain the cocktail from the blender over the crushed ice. Garnish with a wedge of pineapple, a slice of prickly pear or orange, a wedge of lime and a cherry.

Zombie

This legendary 1930s recipe was created at Don the Beachcomber restaurant in Hollywood, reportedly as a hangover cure! It has a long list of ingredients, and yet is a harmonious (and dynamic) mixture.

1 measure/1½ tbsp light rum
½ measure/2 tsp dark rum
½ measure/2 tsp white rum
1 measure/1½ tbsp orange curaçao
¼ measure/1 tsp Pernod
1 measure/1½ tbsp lemon juice
1 measure/1½ tbsp orange juice
1 measure/1½ tbsp pineapple juice
½ measure/2 tsp papaya juice
¼ measure/1 tsp grenadine
½ measure/2 tsp Orgeat (almond syrup)
¼ measure/1 tsp overproof rum

Blend all but the last ingredient with ice, and strain into an ice-packed highball glass. Sprinkle with overproof rum. Garnish with a slice of pineapple, lime and a cherry.

La Bomba

This explosive mixture has more than a touch of the Zombie about it.

1 measure/1½ tbsp light rum
½ measure/2 tsp orange curaçao
½ measure/2 tsp anisette
½ measure/2 tsp apricot brandy
½ measure/2 tsp lemon juice

Shake all the ingredients well with ice, and strain into a chilled cocktail glass. The drink could be garnished with a couple of chunks of pineapple and a maraschino cherry on a cocktail stick.

Piña Colada

This has to be one of the most popular cocktails worldwide, with a name meaning "strained pineapple". For that extra Caribbean touch, the drink may be served in a hollowed-out pineapple shell, which also means that you can liquidize the flesh for the juice in the recipe, but a bowl-shaped cocktail glass is the next best thing.

2 measures/3 tbsp white rum
2 measures/3 tbsp pineapple juice
1½ measures/2 tbsp coconut cream
5ml/1 tsp caster (superfine) sugar
(if freshly blended fruit is used)

Shake all the ingredients well with ice, and strain into a cocktail goblet. Garnish with a slice of pineapple, slices of coconut and a cherry.

Monkey Wrench

Deliciously refreshing, despite its indelicate name, this makes a fine drink for a summer afternoon in the garden.

1½ measures/2 tbsp white rum
3 measures/4½ tbsp grapefruit
  juice
3 measures/4½ tbsp sparkling
  lemonade

Half-fill a highball glass with roughly cracked ice, and add the rum and grapefruit juice. Stir briskly, before topping up with the sparkling lemonade. Decorate with intertwined twists of grapefruit and lemon rind in a suitably artistic arrangement.

Bartending know-how
Never shake anything sparkling, whether lemonade or champagne, as it will only flatten the drink.

Hustler

This is a sharply tangy drink. I prefer it without sugar to emphasize its bite, but around 5ml/1 tsp will not go amiss, if you find it just too sour without.

1 measure/1½ tbsp light rum
1 measure/1½ tbsp white rum
1 measure/1½ tbsp passion fruit juice
juice of a lime
5ml/1 tsp caster (superfine) sugar (optional)

Shake all the ingredients well with ice (especially well to dissolve the sugar if you are using it), and strain into a large wine goblet. Add the empty shell of the lime to the drink.

Escape Route

Punt e Mes, made by the Carpano company of Turin, is one of the classic vermouth brands, and is a must for this elegant cocktail.

1 measure/1½ tbsp light rum
1 measure/1½ tbsp Punt e Mes
½ measure/2 tsp crème de fraise
4 measures/6 tbsp sparkling
*   lemonade*

Half-fill a highball glass with cracked ice, and add the first three ingredients. Stir vigorously before topping up with the lemonade. Garnish with a slice of lemon and a couple of mint leaves.

Bartending know-how
Crème de fraise is a strawberry flavoured creme liqueur. Crème liqueurs (not to be confused with cream liqueurs, made with a spirit base, cream and flavourings) are so named due to their very high levels of sugar, which provides a texture like cream.

Costa del Sol

This is a light, sweet, fizzy drink with a gentle flavour, one of the less tastebud-startling rum cocktails.

2 measures/3 tbsp white rum
1 measure/1½ tbsp sweet red vermouth
1 measure/1½ tbsp sugar syrup
½ measure/2 tsp lemon juice
3 measures/4½ tbsp soda water

Half-fill a highball glass with cracked ice, and then add the first four ingredients. Stir, before adding the soda. Garnish with a lemon twist on a cocktail stick.

Goldilocks

The name is a rough approximation of the final colour of this appealing fruit-juice cocktail.

1 measure/1½ tbsp dark rum
1 measure/1½ tbsp Malibu
3 measures/4½ tbsp pineapple juice
2 measures/3 tbsp orange juice

Shake with ice, and strain into a tall glass half-filled with cracked ice. Garnish with slices of pineapple and orange.

Bartending know-how
Malibu is from Jamaica but its white rum base comes from the island of Barbados.

Sun City

A similar type of blend to the Mai Tai, and almost as lethal, this is a drink with plenty of personality.

1 measure/1½ tbsp white rum
½ measure/2 tsp dark rum
½ measure/2 tsp Galliano
½ measure/2 tsp apricot brandy
2 measures/3 tbsp pineapple juice
¼ measure/1 tsp lime juice
3 measures/4½ tbsp sparkling
*   lemonade*

Shake all but the last ingredient with ice, and then strain into a highball glass. Top up with the lemonade. Garnish with slices of lemon and lime.

Passion Punch

Although it is not really a punch at all, the combination of passion fruit and grape juices in this recipe is a winning one. The acidity of the one is mitigated by the sweetness of the other, with the pineapple syrup adding a viscous texture to the drink.

1½ measures/2 tbsp light rum
1 measure/1½ tbsp red grape juice
1 measure/1½ tbsp passion fruit
    juice
¼ measure/1 tsp pineapple syrup
    (from a can)

Shake all the ingredients well with ice, and strain into a rocks glass.

Beach Peach

The flavour of this cocktail is largely derived from pure, thick peach nectar, and the drink has a nice balance of sweet and sharp flavours. It tastes alluring when sipped on the beach.

1½ measures/2 tbsp white rum
¾ measure/1 tbsp peach brandy
1 measure/1½ tbsp peach nectar
½ measure/2 tsp lime juice
¼ measure/1 tsp sugar syrup

Shake all the ingredients well with ice, and strain into a rocks glass half-filled with cracked ice. Garnish with a slice of ripe peach and a maraschino cherry.

Habanera

Based on a Cuban recipe of the 1940s, which would have used the island's own golden rum, Habanera offers a beguiling combination of chocolate and lime flavours. It's a short but delicious drink that may well have you wanting a second one.

1¾ measures/2½ tbsp of light rum
½ measure/2 tsp brown crème de cacao
juice of half a lime

Shake all the ingredients well with ice, and strain into a cocktail glass. Garnish with a half-slice of lime.

Bartending know-how
Recipes based on white rum are far more interesting if made with one of the small producers' island rums, rather than one of the big multinational proprietary products.

Mojito

A favourite tipple of Ernest Hemingway, this Cuban highball cocktail has become insanely popular over the last few years.

juice of one lime, freshly squeezed, plus extra wedges to garnish
5ml/1 tsp sugar
5 mint leaves, plus extra to garnish
1 measure/1½ tbsp white rum
3 measures/4½ tbsp soda water

In the bottom of a collins glass muddle together the lime juice and sugar. Add the mint leaves and squish them against the side of the glass to release their aromatics. Fill the glass two-thirds full with ice and pour over the rum. Add in the squeezed-out lime shell plus extra wedges and top up with soda water. Garnish with mint leaves.

Jamaica Sunday

A spoonful of honey adds sweetness and an exotic note to this cocktail, the name of which indicates that it should specifically be made with a good Jamaican brand of rum. The darker and stronger the brand, the better.

2 measures/3 tbsp dark rum
¼ measure/1 tsp acacia honey
½ measure/2 tsp lime juice
2 measures/3 tbsp sparkling
   lemonade

In a separate glass, stir the honey into the dark rum until it is dissolved. Half-fill a rocks glass with cracked ice, and then add the honey-rum mixture and the lime juice, and stir again. Add the lemonade. Garnish with lime slices.

Angel's Treat

The addition of cocoa powder to the mixture makes this an unusual but successful recipe. It should be sieved to remove any lumps, and combines very well with the almond-paste flavour of amaretto.

1½ measures/2 tbsp dark rum
1 measure/1½ tbsp Disaronno
  Amaretto
1½ measures/2 tbsp double
  (heavy) cream
2.5ml/½ tsp cocoa powder

Shake all the ingredients very vigorously with ice to dissolve the cocoa, and strain into a bowl-shaped cocktail glass or champagne saucer. Sprinkle the surface with grated dark chocolate.

Hurricane

There are almost as many different recipes for a drink called Hurricane as there are cocktail books, but this particular one, with its exuberantly fruity character, is my favourite.

1½ measures/2 tbsp dark rum
1 measure/1½ tbsp white rum
1 measure/1½ tbsp lime juice
2 measures/3 tbsp passion fruit
   juice
1 measure/1½ tbsp pineapple juice
1 measure/1½ tbsp orange juice
½ measure/2 tsp blackcurrant
   syrup (from a can of fruit)

Shake all the ingredients well with ice, and strain into a highball glass. Decorate with slices of pineapple and orange and a maraschino cherry.

Emerald Star

Despite the presence of the green melon liqueur, the colour of this drink isn't exactly emerald. It's a pretty name nonetheless.

1 measure/1½ tbsp white rum
⅔ measure/1 tbsp Midori
⅓ measure/1½ tsp apricot brandy
⅓ measure/1½ tsp lime juice
1 measure/1½ tbsp passion fruit juice

Shake all the ingredients well with ice, and strain into a cocktail glass. Garnish with a slice of star fruit.

Rum Sidecar

Although the original Sidecar is made with cognac, here's a version of the basic mix that uses light or golden rum. It produces a very slightly sweeter final result.

1½ measures/2 tbsp light rum
¾ measure/1 tbsp Cointreau
¾ measure/1 tbsp lemon juice

Shake all the ingredients well with ice, and strain into a cocktail glass. Garnish with a half-slice of lemon.

Chop Nut

An ingenious blend of coconut, chocolate and hazelnut flavours, all sharpened up with orange, this is a most satisfying drink.

1 measure/1½ tbsp white rum
¾ measure/3 tsp Malibu
½ measure/2 tsp white crème de cacao
¼ measure/1 tsp Frangelico
1½ measures/2 tbsp mandarin juice

Shake all the ingredients well with ice, and strain into a bowl-shaped cocktail glass. For a slightly frothier texture, add 5ml/1 tsp egg white as well. Garnish with a twist of mandarin rind.

Petite Fleur

This tangy, refreshing cocktail makes a good aperitif. I'm not sure what flower is meant to be invoked by its name. Perhaps you can decide as you drink it.

1 measure/1½ tbsp white rum
1 measure/1½ tbsp Cointreau
1 measure/1½ tbsp grapefruit juice

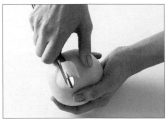

Shake all the ingredients well with ice, and strain into a cocktail glass. Add a twist of grapefruit rind.

Poker

Here is a simple cocktail from the 1920s. The preference now is for the proportions given below, although it was originally half-and-half. It may also be made with light rum instead of white, if you prefer.

1½ measures/2 tbsp white rum
¾ measure/1 tbsp sweet red
  vermouth

Shake the ingredients well with ice, and strain into a cocktail glass. Squeeze a twist of orange rind over the surface of the drink to release a spray of oil and then drop it in.

Rompope

Legend has it that this rich egg-nog was first made in the kitchens of a convent in Puebla, Mexico. It is traditional to seal bottles of Rompope with rolled corn husks, or corn cobs that have been stripped of their corn. The recipe makes 1.5 litres/2½ pints, and will keep for up to one week in the refrigerator.

1 litre/1¾ pints milk
350g/12oz sugar
2.5ml/½ tsp bicarbonate of soda
  (baking soda)
1 cinnamon stick
12 large egg yolks
300ml/½ pint dark rum

Pour the milk into a pan and stir in the sugar and bicarbonate of soda. Add the cinnamon stick. Place the pan over a medium heat and bring the mixture to the boil, stirring constantly. Immediately pour the mixture into a bowl and cool to room temperature. Remove the cinnamon stick, squeezing it gently to release any liquid.

Put the egg yolks in a heatproof bowl over a pan of simmering water and whisk until the mixture is very thick and pale. Add the whisked yolks to the milk mixture a little at a time, beating after each addition.

Return the mixture to a clean pan, and cook gently until the mixture thickens and the back of the spoon is visible when a finger is drawn along it. Stir in the rum, pour into sterilized bottles and seal tightly with stoppers. Chill until required, and serve very cold.

Morning Joy

One wouldn't necessarily recommend making a habit of these, but the idea is of a more robust approach than usual to the glass of breakfast juice. How much joy it spreads over the morning may well depend on how joyful the night before was.

1½ measures/2 tbsp light rum
6 measures/135ml/4½fl oz
   grapefruit juice
¼ measure/1 tsp sloe gin

Half-fill a highball glass with cracked ice, and then add the ingredients in this order, sprinkling the sloe gin on top as a float.

X.Y.Z.

The significance of its mysterious algebraic name escapes me, but this is a 1920s recipe that has survived the test of time. It's a strong one too.

2 measures/3 tbsp dark rum
1 measure/1½ tbsp Cointreau
1 measure/1½ tbsp lemon juice

Shake all the ingredients well with ice, and strain into a large cocktail glass. Add a half-slice of lemon.

Trade Winds

The correct rum brand to use for this cocktail is Mount Gay, made on Barbados. It is properly served frappé.

2 measures/3 tbsp light rum
½ measure/2 tsp slivovitz
½ measure/2 tsp lime juice
½ measure/2 tsp Orgeat (almond syrup)

Shake the ingredients well with ice, and strain into a cocktail glass filled with crushed ice. Add a half-slice of lime.

Bartending know-how
Orgeat syrup is a useful addition to your cocktail bar. It is versatile, has a great almond flavour and mixes well with many cocktails. A mere dash will give the flavour you require; any more would oversweeten the drink.

Continental

An old-fashioned mixture of rum and peppermint cordial was once a popular drink. This cocktail presents a more adventurous spin on that formula. The colour is an attractive shade of green, and the mint flavour is agreeably set off by the piercing note of lime.

1½ measures/2 tbsp light rum
½ measure/2 tsp green crème de menthe
½ measure/2 tsp lime juice

Shake all the ingredients well with ice, and strain into a cocktail glass. If available, add a sprig of mint to the drink.

Bolero

Here is one of those cocktails that's all alcohol and no mixers. Stirring the drink gently, as opposed to shaking it, emphasizes its strength, in the sense that the mixture doesn't become quite as chilled as it would in the shaker.

1½ measures/2 tbsp light rum
¾ measure/1 tbsp calvados
¼ measure/1 tsp sweet red
  vermouth

Mix the ingredients gently in a pitcher with a couple of ice cubes, and then strain into a pre-chilled rocks glass. Squeeze a twist of lemon over the drink, and then drop it in.

Kingston

This is named after the Jamaican capital, so it would be inappropriate to use rum from any other location.

1½ measures/2 tbsp dark Jamaica
* rum*
¾ measure/1 tbsp gin
juice of half a lime
¼ measure/1 tsp grenadine

Shake all the ingredients well with ice, and strain into a cocktail glass. Garnish with a half-slice of lime.

Bartending know-how
Grenadine, or grenadine syrup, is made from the juice of pomegranates. It has a rich ruby red colour and a very sweet flavour. Its distinctive red colouring and sweet taste make it a popular ingredient in a wide variety of cocktails.

San Juan

A coconutty, fruity and strong cocktail seems the only fitting way to celebrate the sun-soaked capital of Puerto Rico.

1½ measures/2 tbsp light rum
1 measure/1½ tbsp grapefruit juice
1 measure/1½ tbsp lime juice
½ measure/2 tsp coconut cream
¼ measure/1 tsp overproof dark
    rum

Blend all except the last ingredient with cracked ice in the liquidizer, and then pour into a bowl-shaped cocktail glass. Sprinkle the surface of the drink with the overproof rum, and add a half-slice of lime.

Green Caribbean

One of the 1980s creations that accompanied the launch of the delectable Japanese melon liqueur Midori, the name of which simply means "green". It's a supremely refreshing long drink with an appreciable kick.

1½ measures/2 tbsp white rum
1½ measures/2 tbsp Midori
4 measures/6 tbsp soda water

Shake the first two ingredients with ice, and strain into a highball glass. Add the soda and a half-slice of lemon.

Bartending know-how
Midori was launched at Studio 54 in New York in 1978 during a party held by the cast, crew and producers of the movie *Saturday Night Fever*.

Jamaican Black Coffee

There are any number of combinations of alcohol with hot brewed coffee, some more successful than others. This delicious version of black coffee is in fact only slightly alcoholic but gains extra allure from the inclusion of citrus fruits. The recipe serves eight.

1 lemon and 2 oranges, finely sliced
1.5 litres/2½ pints black coffee
  (filter/cafetière brewed using
  55g/2oz coffee per 1 litre/
  1¾ pints water)
2 measures/3 tbsp light rum
85g/3oz caster (superfine) sugar

Place the lemon and orange slices in a pan. Add the coffee and heat. When the mixture is about to boil, pour in the rum and sugar, stirring well until the sugar dissolves, then immediately remove from the heat. While the coffee is still very hot, pour or ladle into heatproof glasses, and garnish with a fresh lemon slice.

Hot Tea Toddy

Rum isn't just a good partner for coffee. It also goes unexpectedly well with tea. Use a good Indian leaf, such as Assam or Darjeeling in this recipe, and strain it.

1½ measures/2 tbsp light rum
2.5ml/½ tsp clear honey
2.5ml/½ tsp ground cinnamon
slice of lemon
1 teacup hot black tea
piece of crystallized (candied) ginger

Add all but the ginger to a pan and gently warm until just about to boil. Pour into a mug and add the ginger.

Bartending know-how
Hot tea cocktails are pretty few and far between. Use a fairly straightforward blend such as English Breakfast tea or perhaps Assam or Darjeeling.

Index

This edition is published by Lorenz Books, an imprint of Anness Publishing Ltd
info@anness.com
twitter: @AnnessLorenzBks
www.annesspublishing.com

© Anness Publishing Ltd 2018

A CIP catalogue record for this book is available from the British Library.

Publisher: Joanna Lorenz
Editorial Director: Helen Sudell
Photographers: Frank Adam, Steve Baxter, Janine Hosegood, Jon Whitaker
Designer: Nigel Partridge
Production Controller: Ben Worley

PUBLISHER'S NOTE
Although the advice and information in this book are believed to be accurate and true at the time of going to press, neither the authors nor the publisher can accept any legal responsibility or liability for any errors or omissions that may have been made nor for any loss, harm or injury that comes about from following instructions or advice in this book.

DRINK AWARENESS
Always drink legally and responsibly. Do not drink and drive, and avoid alcohol whilst pregnant or trying to conceive.